IMAGES
of America

DENHAM SPRINGS

ON THE COVER: The Lively and Bauer families pose with a new car in 1924. One of the Livelys, the owner, sits behind the steering wheel. One of the first automobiles purchased in Denham Springs, it is seen in front of the Livelys' land along Range Avenue.

IMAGES of America
DENHAM SPRINGS

PJ Oubre on behalf of Old City Hall

Copyright © 2013 by PJ Oubre on behalf of Old City Hall
ISBN 978-1-5316-6833-4

Published by Arcadia Publishing
Charleston, South Carolina

Library of Congress Control Number: 2013933922

For all general information, please contact Arcadia Publishing:
Telephone 843-853-2070
Fax 843-853-0044
E-mail sales@arcadiapublishing.com
For customer service and orders:
Toll-Free 1-888-313-2665

Visit us on the Internet at www.arcadiapublishing.com

Contents

Acknowledgments		6
Introduction		7
1.	Early Settlement	9
2.	Baptisms and Burials	37
3.	Public Service and Public Works	53
4.	Classrooms and Characters	69
5.	Off to Work, Off to War	87
6.	Parks and Recreation	103
7.	Commerce and Development	111

Acknowledgments

The author would like to thank the director of Old City Hall in Denham Springs, Patti Peairs; without her openness, this book would never have existed. Also, a thanks goes to Kathleen Dawkins at Old City Hall; without her willingness to contact local families and promote my project, I would never have completed this book. Unless otherwise noted, all photographs appear courtesy of Old City Hall.

I am greatly indebted to the members of our community that answered my calls for research and images and offered their support. These wonderful and patient individuals cheerfully responded to my constant phone calls and innumerable questions.

I want to extend my gratitude to the staff at Arcadia Publishing, especially my editor, Jason Humphrey, for his tireless support and constant positivity throughout this project. I need to thank Matt Magnuson and St. James Technologies for the loan of their photography equipment so that I could capture high-quality images of Denham Springs as it looks today and Isral Duke for his time and energy in assisting me in taking and processing photographs, as well as his unyielding support.

Finally, I want to extend my greatest gratefulness to my loving wife, Katie, whose love, support, and inexhaustible patience have made me the man that I am today. Her encouragement and devotion are the reasons I decided to embark on this glorious adventure.

INTRODUCTION

As the largest commercial and residential municipality in Livingston Parish, Denham Springs has a rich story that speaks of its diversity and uniqueness as a city in southeast Louisiana. The city has risen from a village of farmers and cattle ranchers located on the Amite River into an economic beacon for the entire parish to look toward for guidance into the 21st century.

Originally settled in 1755, Denham Springs was a collection of farmers and planters who lived along the banks of the Amite River. The source of attraction to early settlers was both the river and the mineral springs that provided potable water. The springs produced pure water that was noticeably different from any other water source in Louisiana.

The first settler in the area was Alexander Hogue, a Scotsman from Georgia. Hogue arrived in 1804, and the only documents that have survived are the land claims with his name attached. Another pioneer and founder of Denham Springs was John Noblet, who was Hogue's neighbor, living on the banks of the Amite River.

William Denham, a native of Wilkinson County, Mississippi, arrived in 1828 and settled in the area. As a neighbor of Hogue, the two men became friends, and Denham married Hogue's daughter Mercy Hogue. Following their wedding, Denham purchased the land from Hogue and settled with his bride. A popular myth states that William Denham discovered the mineral springs on his property. According to the 1850 census, Denham's occupation was listed as "farmer," highlighting the agricultural foundations of Denham Springs.

As the years progressed, more settlers came to the area, and on May 1, 1855, Denham sold his land claims to Stamaty Covas, an Irish lawyer from New Orleans, for $3,050. Denham and his family moved to Baton Rouge and later to Texas.

During the antebellum period under the ownership of Covas, a health resort developed near the mineral springs. The hamlet was known as Amite Springs, which would later be renamed to Hill's Springs and finally Denham Springs. An article in a Baton Rouge newspaper describes a bridge built of boats across the river to the springs at Amite Springs.

Following the Civil War, Covas went delinquent on his taxes and lost the land, which George Livingston Minton had purchased in 1882 for $124. This was the amount of the delinquent taxes owed by Covas. Minton promoted the regenerative and restorative properties of the springs, and under his leadership a resort reemerged with several hotels operating near the springs on the banks of the river. Parish conveyance records indicate that Minton began subdividing the land for residential and commercial use.

John Sullivan filed an application to establish a post office in 1879, which was built north of city limits. The location given was one mile south of Beaver Creek and east of the Amite River. Confusion had continued to gather concerning the name of the town at that time. When it was established in 1880, the given name was Hill's Springs. In 1890, when John Allen became postmaster, the office relocated within city limits, and in 1898 the name was changed to Denham Springs. The post office department made the change, presumably because of other Louisiana communities with similar names.

Minton eventually became the first mayor in 1903 and established the local newspaper *Denham Springs News* as the town continued to develop following its incorporation. Denham Springs witnessed the establishment of several schools, including the renowned Denham Springs Collegiate Institute, and doctors, lawyers, and banks began operations. Even while facing several significant floods, the town continued to grow and saw the additions of the east-west US Highway 190 to the south of the town center and Interstate 12, much farther south, in the 1970s.

The completion of the Baton Rouge, Hammond and Eastern Railroad line spawned a shift in the city center to Range Avenue. The first train ran in 1908, and businesses began to prosper along this east-west rail line. Denham Springs became a hub for farmers, and cargo traffic from all around Livingston Parish found its way on the frequent trains that stopped in town.

The construction of the interstate led to a shift southward as businesses and hotels opened along this highway. The city center experienced a downturn throughout the 1970s and 1980s, until the Main Street Association stepped in and provided a renewed campaign of business and historic preservation. Now the city hosts many attractions and businesses. The best known and prominent of all the developments in Denham Springs is the Historic Antiques & Art District, which attracts visitors across the nation to shop for days. The district features over 20 antique, art, and boutique shops. In addition, people come from all around the state to visit one of the largest Bass Pro Shops and take time to explore the wonderful parks and businesses downtown.

One
Early Settlement

Jule E. Felder poses with his wife, Olive Miscar Felder, at the Art Parlors, located in Baton Rouge, in 1927. Many families in the early years of the city often traveled to Baton Rouge for the rare opportunity to have a photograph taken for their family memory books.

Pictured here in 1899 is Leoma "Fridge" Lively, one of several early matriarchs to raise a family in the early years of Denham Springs.

This photograph, taken in 1927, is of Eduardo H. Douglass of Denham Springs.

Leo Miscar (left) and Arthur Clement pose in front of the Clement farmhouse along River Road in 1922. Miscar hauled cattle for locals to the stockyards. As a cattle rancher, he served every family in the early years of the town.

Josephine Thibodeaux Sides is pictured at her family's farm in Denham Springs in 1908. Josephine was married to John Sides.

Leslie Clement rides his horse on his farm, located in the southern part of town. His was typical of the many cattle ranches and farms that spanned the south part of Denham Springs.

This is a photograph of the Miscar farm in Denham Springs in 1916. Denham Springs was comprised of several family farms until the first paved highway through town was established.

Lois Felder Benton and her husband, Charlie Benton, were reunited in 1945 after Benton returned from serving in World War II.

This is a photograph of Rosa Miscar Watkins, taken in 1911. She was the mother of Ora and Gertrude Watkins. The Watkins family continues to live in Denham Springs today.

Pictured here are members of the Miscar family: Harvey Warren Miscar, Elizabeth Lively Miscar, and their two children, Dewey and Rosa. This photograph was taken in 1909.

Dr. Bonner Duke was a Civil War physician who arrived in the springs in 1890. He and Dr. Montgomery Williams started a practice together around 1910 from this house on Main Street. This was a boardinghouse for traveling and new doctors in the area. Later, Duke and Williams examined patients at the nearby Robinson Clinic on Main Street.

The Springs Hotel opened on June 8, 1906 and was one of the first local establishments for lodging in the area. The hotel capitalized on opportunities presented by travelers from Baton Rouge and the surrounding area. Many of these travelers crossed the nearby Amite River at Benton's Ferry. The hotel overlooked a public flow well that provided drinking water to local citizens and their horses. Locals would often stop and visit the hotel to inquire about visitors before collecting water from the flow well and returning to their homes. (Courtesy of Jill Benton Glass.)

Cecil Benton tends his personal garden after years of farming. He is seen outside of his house on Cedar Street in the 1940s. (Courtesy of Donna Benton.)

Clinton Allen was a local businessman who owned a great deal of land north of Denham Springs. Clinton Allen Road was named after him because he owned and subdivided most of the farmland in that area between Arnold and Cane Market Roads.

Joseph Louis Sanchez poses here with his hunting dog and rifle. Sanchez was one of the early members of the Denham Springs Hunting Club. (Courtesy of the Sanchez family.)

This is a 1920 photograph of Dr. G.W. Jones and his family. Jones, standing in the center, served the people of Denham Springs for over 30 years. Seated on the far left is his son Julius Jones, who served as mayor from 1926 to 1930.

Cyrus Luther "Panny" Tucker was one of the more animated and colorful characters of the community. He was born into the Tucker family, who moved to Denham Springs from Clio.

Featured here are James Washington Andrews and his wife, Bell Weathersby Andrews. Note the fashion of the day in this c. 1900 photograph. (Courtesy of Carol Lamm.)

Evelyn Marsh Benton stands in front of the Amite River holding her son Cecil. The Benton family is a large and expansive one, with most relatives descending from the first Benton to arrive in Denham Springs: Robert Benton. (Courtesy of Donna Benton.)

Cecil and Evelyn Benton sit atop the first truck owned in Denham Springs in 1914. (Courtesy of Donna Benton.)

Brothers Billy (left) and Cecil Benton pose here on the side of Hummel Street in the 1940s. Hummel Street had not yet been paved, as documented by the dirt road. (Courtesy of Donna Benton.)

The Smiley and Tucker families left the village of Clio in 1906 and moved to the recently incorporated town of Denham Springs. The people posing here are ancestors of many influential families living in the city today. (Courtesy of Linda Fugler May.)

Here are two photographs of the same couple 40 years apart. The image to the left of Walter Miller and Augusta Tucker Miller was captured after their marriage in 1908. They met during Augusta's family's move from Clio to Denham Springs. Walter was operating a ferry at nearby Port Vincent and ferried Augusta and her family across the river. These two had 13 children and have many descendants living today. (Courtesy Ann Fugler.)

Powers Drug Store was a popular stop for children after school. Members of the Denham Springs High School class of 1922 stand outside of the drugstore and pose for a photograph in 1922.

This is a portrait of Oscar Montgomery, son of Victoria Miscar Griffin. Very little is known of Montgomery, but the c. 1932 photograph demonstrates fashion trends of gentlemen during the Great Depression.

Olive Miscar poses in front of Livingston Motors in 1927. The business was located on Centerville Street across from the old Easterly Street.

Wiley Sharp was the son of former sheriff Simpson Sharp. Wiley is seen here in front of Powers Drug Store in 1922.

Bill and Birdie Barnett stand in front of an oil well located on their property. Bill was a prominent businessman and later opened and operated Barnett's Grocery Store. Birdie was a Miller before marrying Bill, and their son Billy Barnett later owned Brignac Dodge with his wife, Jean Brignac Barnett.

This is a photograph of Ora (left) and Gertrude Watkins, who were the daughters of Rosa Miscar Watkins. The two girls are pictured in their childhood around 1928.

Born in Texas, William Brown came to Denham Springs in 1908 on a bicycle from Baton Rouge. He had acquired the skills and knowledge of all oar-making trades. He opened Brown's Oar Factory, along with Jim Benton, near the railroad tracks. Pictured here are his son Jim Brown, Jim's wife Eunice, and their three children.

Sammie Brecheen Benton, born in 1905, was a prominent matriarch of the Benton family. She served as a flower girl around 1910 during the first wedding conducted in the sanctuary at First Baptist Church. (Courtesy of Cissy Benton Waldrep.)

Leslie N. Benton married Sammie Brecheen Benton (pictured) in 1917. They had six children, several of which opened and operated Benton Brothers Furniture. (Courtesy of Cissy Benton Waldrep.)

The Benton Hotel, built in 1912, was originally owned and operated by Jim Benton. It had 12 rooms and housed a local dentist office and a café on the ground floor. William Brown purchased the hotel in 1927 and renamed it Brown Hotel. Brown owned Brown's Oar Factory, which was located behind the hotel. He used scrap lumber from the factory as heating fuel for the hotel. (Courtesy of Cissy Benton Waldrep.)

Julius Jones Sr. drives a horse-drawn wagon at the corner of Centerville and Third Streets in front of the family funeral home around 1875. This is a classic image of life in Denham Springs in the 19th century. (Courtesy of Cissy Benton Waldrep.)

The Watson Hotel featured 21 rooms and was built on land that once occupied the Denham Hotel before it burned down. A.B. Easterly built the Watson Hotel in 1899 and prospered by constructing several hotels, including the famous Springs Hotel. (Courtesy of Cissy Benton Waldrep.)

Hazel Freeman (standing, left) and Gladys (standing, right) and Evelyn Marsh have fun in the backyard in 1928. These ladies represent the fun and vibrant attitude that continues to exists in the community today. (Courtesy of Donna Benton.)

Photographed here are Annie Laura Miller Fugler (left) and her brother Boyd Walter Miller. This image shows the typical style of clothes worn by young children in the 1920s.

This is an image of Benjamin Franklin Fugler Jr. standing in front of the Fugler house in 1938. He was born in 1909 in the village of Watson, located north of Denham Springs.

The early family of J.E. "Pet" Garrison poses here in 1913. J.E. was Livingston Parish's first county agent in 1912. Featured in this photograph are Gracie Garrison Tucker (standing, left), Winona Garrison Felder (standing, right), Jesse L. Garrison (seated, left), J.E. Garrison, and Annie Belle Garrison holding Beatrice Garrison Bardwell. Although they had more children after this photograph was taken, this simple family was connected to many other early families in the community by the marriage of their children. Many of these families still live in Denham Springs.

The mineral springs were reported to have restorative properties that attracted many patients from Baton Rouge and New Orleans. Seen here are two women drinking from one of the many springs that still exist in Denham Springs.

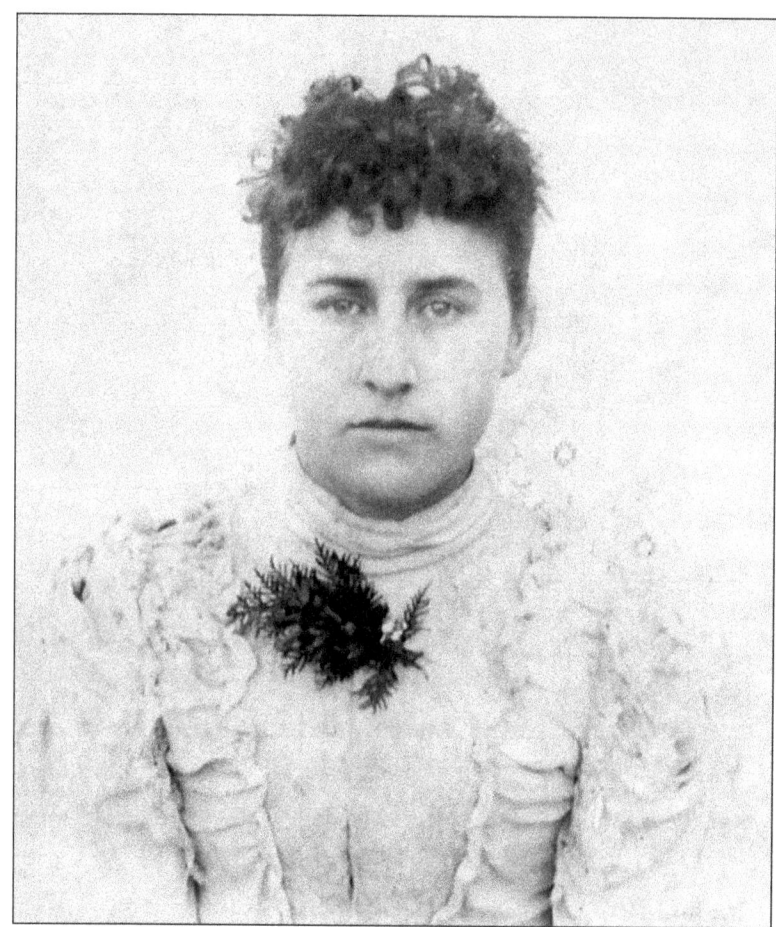

Lois Sarah Harris, one of several wealthy housewives in Denham Springs, had this image taken in Baton Rouge in 1909. It is a perfect example of the latest in women's fashion at the turn of the 20th century. (Courtesy of Robbie Spangler.)

The station agent's house, built in 1911, was conveniently located near the rail yard and train station.

In June 1904, fifteen Master Masons gathered from the area and signed a petition to establish a new lodge in Denham Springs. They were successful, and Lodge no. 297 opened a year later in 1905. The Masons continue to thrive today, although in a new building. (Courtesy of the Louisiana Masonic Library and Museum.)

Alexander Hogue was one of the first settlers of Denham Springs. This is a photograph of his land claim, which he sold to his son-in-law William Denham in 1828. The claim is for the 640-acre tract of land. Denham Springs was named after William Denham many years later.

Edward Coleman Benton, a local blacksmith, owned one of the largest farms along what is now Range Avenue, south of the city center. He is seen here before heading to church service at First Baptist Church.

Two

Baptisms and Burials

The First Baptist Church was located on the corner of Centerville Street and River Road. This photograph of the second sanctuary was taken from the parking lot across the street from River Road. The first sanctuary was destroyed by an Amite River flood and was built higher than its predecessor.

The First Baptist Church conducted a large choir and trained many classes of schoolchildren through the years. Here, a group of children boards the bus for a choir trip in 1967. (Courtesy of Gwen Miller Willis.)

More volunteers work on the foundation of the Amite Church. This project was a massive undertaking, and the outpouring of volunteers was the largest the city had seen. Wives came out to bring lemonade to their husbands and assist in any way they could.

This is a photograph of the first sanctuary for the First Baptist Church in 1900. The church, started by Rev. H.T. Comish, who came to Louisiana in 1884, was established on May 6, 1900, and Comish was its first minister. Seen in the far right background is the old Benton House.

Virgil Seale Sr. founded Seale Funeral Home, located on the corner of Main Street and North College Avenue, in 1957. He established his funeral home on the tenets of honesty and fairness in dealing with the remains of deceased members of local families. The Seales conducted an open house, inviting the community to visit their new property on September 14 and 15, 1957. Seale Funeral Home still serves the community and is now located on Range Avenue just north of Interstate 12.

Billy G. Seale was cofounder of Seale Funeral Home. The marketing tagline for his funeral home was "Seale Funeral Service is manned by friendly experienced personnel who are your friends and neighbors."

Seale Funeral Home continues to serve the communities of Livingston Parish. Pictured here in front of the current building are, from left to right, Billy Seale, Stacy Seale, and L.W. "Mickey" Seale.

Pictured is the first Seale Funeral Service building, where a Seale open house was held in 1957. The company served the town of Denham Springs here until the relocation to Range Avenue, south of the town center.

Seen here is the front entrance to the current location of Seale Funeral Home. The move southward from the city center was an indication of how the city would develop around the newly constructed Interstate 12 in the 1970s. The city began to shift southward in the 1980s and 1990s.

Denham Springs Catholic Chapel was erected in 1914. The Diocese of Baton Rouge sent Fr. John Anthony Heil of St. George Catholic Church once a month to give Holy Mass to the minor Catholic members of the community in Denham Springs. (Courtesy of Diocese of Baton Rouge Department of Archives.)

The chapel car St. Paul traveled to rural communities along railroad track lines throughout the United States to shepherd local Catholic communities that did not yet possess a church. This is a converted passenger car given by a private donor; it arrived in Denham Springs on March 16, 1918, and remained for six days. (Courtesy of Diocese of Baton Rouge Department of Archives.)

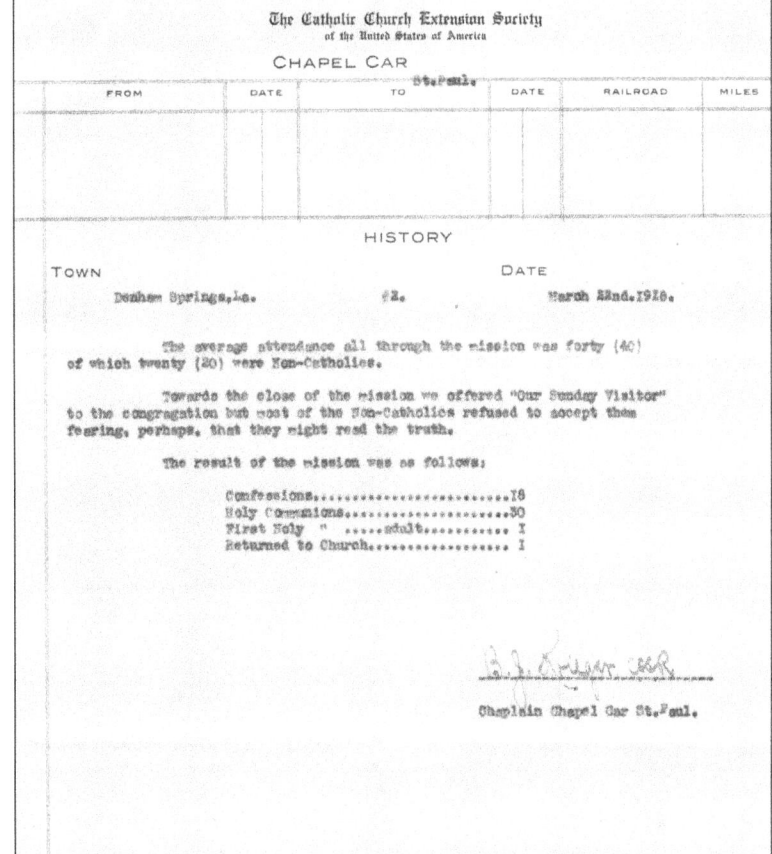

The chaplain of the chapel car St. Paul recorded the schedule of sacramental events and attendance during his six-day stay in Denham Springs. (Courtesy of Diocese of Baton Rouge Department of Archives.)

The third sanctuary seen here currently stands and serves the Baptist members of Denham Springs. The current First Baptist Church was erected on the corner of Centerville Street and River Road.

Established on October 9, 1841, a group of believers drafted a constitution and founded the Amite Baptist Church. Located north of Denham Springs on Amite Church Road, it is the host church to one of the oldest cemeteries in the city.

These images show the Amite Baptist Church cemetery. The earliest burial was January 28, 1858, which occurred 17 years after the founding of the church. Pictured below is the older section of the cemetery, with a second section directly across the street from the front of the sanctuary.

Originally established as a village graveyard for the church, the First Baptist Church Cemetery had its first burial in 1805 with the funeral of Michael Sullivan. The plots were free to anyone who wanted to bury a deceased family member, and the cemetery was operated by the church until it was transferred to the city on February 2, 1955. The first mayor, George L. Minton, was buried here, although his gravestone no longer remains.

Situated beneath tall oak and pine trees at the end of Tabernacle Street near the Amite River was an open tin-roofed tabernacle that had been erected by the Methodist Camp Meeting Association. In 1898, a group of Methodists began meeting there under Rev. J. Martin Alford of Live Oak Methodist Church. Reverend Alford gained permission to organize a Methodist church in Denham Springs. In 1902, a building was erected across Center Street from the tabernacle. Due to the flooding of the Amite River in 1925, the congregation sought higher ground and built a church across the street from the one pictured here on Mattie Street.

The Denham Springs Memorial Cemetery occupies land that was once a strawberry field owned by James Freeman. The town council purchased the land for the cemetery in 1935. The plots were ready for purchase in 1937, and the conversion work was funded by the Works Progress Administration (WPA).

Roberts United Methodist Church is the first and oldest African American church in Denham Springs. Established in 1894, it was originally housed in a log cabin on Cockerham Road. Reverend Woodard established the church and purchased land north of Denham Springs in 1897 to build a new place of worship. (Courtesy of Arthur Perkins.)

The New Zion Baptist Church served the African American community and was established from the Little Zion Baptist Church that moved from Frost, Louisiana, to Denham Springs in 1932. The congregation purchased land and built a new church, which was completed in 1941 and renamed as New Zion Baptist Church under the pastorship of Rev. J.L. Manuel, who was the congregation's minister until his death in 1965. (Courtesy of Arthur Perkins.)

Br. Jack Mason had the idea to start a prayer meeting and group that invited Christians and non-Christians alike in 1925. He invited Rev. J.L. Holiday, and together they put prepared a proposal for a new visionary church. In October 1931, they approached the Amite River Progressive Christian Association, and the Midway Baptist Church was formed and ministered to all congregations, primarily among African American communities. Midway Baptist Church continues to grow under the leadership of Arthur Gilmore. (Courtesy of Arthur Perkins.)

Volunteers in the community work together to pour concrete for the foundation of the Amite Church, facing River Road. (Courtesy of Gerry Kelly.)

High school children pose in front of the First Baptist Church bus. The bus was known as the "Big Blue and White." Here, kids that graduated in 1964 pose before a church choir outing. (Courtesy of David Tillman.)

In the early years of the history of the Catholic community in Denham Springs, Diocesan priests from Baton Rouge traveled across the Amite River to give Mass. The first Catholic church was erected in 1916 to serve the Catholic families. The Church of the Immaculate Conception of the Blessed Virgin Mary was established as a parish on September 11, 1960, when Fr. Joseph Ryan was appointed as its first official pastor. Today, the Church of the Immaculate Conception is located on Hatchell Lane and is overseen by Fr. Frank Uter.

This is a 1900 photograph of the first sanctuary of the First Baptist Church, located at River and Centerville Streets. This is the oldest church that continues to serve the community.

Dr. D. Lewis White leads worship service at the First Baptist Church around 1958. White was pastor of the church for about 10 years. (Courtesy of Jim Spring.)

Three
PUBLIC SERVICE AND PUBLIC WORKS

Deputies of the Denham Springs City Police pose in front of the city hall on Mattie Street, which is now the Old City Hall museum. Taken in 1970, the city police officers pose with Alvin E. Corley, the chief of police, and his secretary Shirley Delaune.

The old fire station was located on the corner of Mattie and Benton Streets, adjacent to Old City Hall. In this 1946 photograph, Leon Jackson poses in front of a fire truck. Dr. T.W. Morgan served as the first fire chief of Denham Springs in 1950. (Courtesy of Penn Morgan.)

Seated around a conference table in city hall in 1965 are, from left to right, Robin Hood (alderman), Robert Mellon (city attorney), Matthew Scivique (mayor), Joe Stafford (alderman), V.W. Brignac, and J. Dick Barnett.

George L. Minton served as mayor in 1903, from 1909 to 1912, and again from 1919 to 1922. Minton purchased land for $124 from Stamaty Covas of New Orleans, who was delinquent on his taxes. Minton was the first mayor of Denham Springs and founded the *Denham Springs News*. He was on the board of directors of the Livingston Bank and an active member of Amite Baptist Church. He presided over an ordinance that prohibited false alarms to be reported over telephone wires on February 15, 1912. He died in Denham Springs on March 31, 1927.

John B. Easterly served as mayor in 1904. Easterly built one of the first hotels in the area around the springs. As a successful hotel owner, he capitalized on the popular belief that the springs possessed health and regenerative properties.

Adolphus E. Jones, born in Greensburg, Louisiana, was a local businessman and lawyer. He received his first patent from the US government in May 1893. He briefly served as mayor in 1904. He continued to promote the positive business future that Denham Springs offered to entrepreneurs.

Ivy Cockerham served as mayor from 1904 to 1906. Born in 1840, he owned the Cockerham Hotel, one of the earliest hotels in the resort around the springs. He also served as the Sunday school superintendent at First Baptist Church in Denham Springs and was a charter member of the same church in 1900. He had 12 children and died in 1921.

William Leonidas Jones was born in Amite County, Mississippi, on September 3, 1847. Jones moved to Springfield, Louisiana, during his childhood. After serving in the Louisiana Infantry during the Civil War, he relocated to Denham Springs and married Mary Cockerham. He served four years on the police jury and as superintendent of public education and was elected and served as mayor from 1906 to 1908. He presided over the completion of the Baton Rouge, Hammond and Eastern Railroad line and the construction of the train depot. Jones died in Baton Rouge on October 1, 1930.

Dewitt Brown served as mayor from 1908 to 1909. Here, Brown stands in the doorway to the first post office, located on Stump Street. He was the third postmaster of Denham Springs, which was established in 1880. Originally, the town was named Hill's Springs.

James Milton Smiley served as mayor in 1912, from 1914 to 1919, and once again from 1922 to 1926. He ran unopposed and received 56 votes on April 16, 1912. Smiley was related to the Tucker and Fugler families, who played a significant role in the continuing development of Denham Springs. He was a very prominent citizen serving on the town council and school board and was elected as mayor three times. He was forced to resign in 1912, which caused a special election to be held.

W. Howell Chambers was a prominent merchant, owning a general store and later a grocery store in town. His wife died in 1911 after the two were married for only a few weeks. A year after her death, he served as mayor from November 1912 to December 1912 as the one-month "Thanksgiving" mayor. He served as mayor pro tempore, following Smiley's resignation and a special election. His tenure as mayor survived through the Thanksgiving holiday but ended on December 17, 1912. During his term, he presided over an ordinance that involved licensing butchers and market shops.

James Oldridge Brannon, pictured here, served as mayor from December 1912 to December 1914. Brannon was related by marriage to the Benton family. Brannon ran unopposed in a special election in December 1912 to fill the vacated seat by James Smiley. He received only 17 votes during this special election. He presided over a growing population of 56 (1912) to 192 (1914) people. Louisiana governor L.E. Hall called for a special election for the school board of Livingston Parish during Brannon's term.

James Leonard Westbrook was from Baton Rouge and served as a member of the board of directors of the Bank of Denham Springs before he ran for mayor. He served as mayor from July 1919 to January 1922.

Julius W. Jones was the son of Dr. G.W. Jones. He married Elvira Cockerham and was an agent for Chrysler Automobiles and part owner of Cockerham-Jones Motor Co. He also served as mayor from June 1926 to June 1930.

Edgar Nye Barnett, born in Denham Springs on June 9, 1889, served as mayor from June 1930 to June 1934. He presided over economic hardships due to the Great Depression and struggled to encourage population retention during his term. He died on June 20, 1949.

William Carl Patterson served as mayor from June 12, 1934, to June 22, 1936, and again from June 1946 until October 31, 1948 (Halloween). He was born in Tunnel Hill, Georgia, and married Ima Cockerham of Denham Springs. He was a veteran of World War I and elected alderman of the city before serving twice as mayor.

Gay Cooper served as mayor from May 1937 to June 1942. He was the serving as mayor during the outbreak of World War II and presided over a generation of Denham Springs boys going off to serve in combat. He was an active member of the community, often spending time with the citizens of Denham Springs fishing for catfish in the Amite River.

Paul Tulane Jones was born in Denham Springs on October 19, 1897. He married Eula Coxe and founded Livingston Savings and Loan. He served as mayor from June 1942 to June 1946 and again from November 1948 to June 1950. As mayor, he witnessed many young men drafted and shipped to Europe and the Pacific.

Charles Brignac was a local businessman who owned and operated a chain of automobile dealerships. He was elected as mayor in June 1950 and served until June 1954.

Earnest Easterly Sr. was beloved by many, as he served intermittently as superintendent of schools from 1920 to 1961. His wife, Esna Easterly, was an eighth-grade teacher, and the couple took pride in the education of the children of Denham Springs. He served as mayor of the city from June 1954 to August 1955.

Dixon Allen served as mayor from August 1955 to June 1958.

Pictured here is Shelly O'Neal, who served as mayor from June 1958 to October 1964. O'Neal also served as a city judge during his term as mayor. He resigned in 1964 over business matters, and a special election was held to occupy his vacant seat.

This is Matt A. Scivique, who served as mayor from October 1964 to June 1970. Scivique won a special election to fill the seat vacated by Shelly O'Neal. He won a bid for reelection in 1966 and served the city successfully for six years. He acted as mayor at the beginning of construction of Interstate 12 that ran east-west through Denham Springs.

John O. Burnett served as mayor from June 1970 to June 1974. Burnett served as an alderman, and as mayor he presided over one of the most difficult financial crises in the city's history.

V. Herbert Hoover served as mayor from June 1974 to December 1990. He was the longest-serving mayor of Denham Springs. He was dedicated and capable, planning and committing to every project he presided over. He shied away from public displays of honor or glory. He oversaw the most fiscally responsible years at city hall. Hoover served during trying times for the city, and he was so influential that the road on which the city court is located is named Mayor Herbert Hoover Avenue.

James E. Delaune was a lawyer and supporter of local business and historic preservation. He served as mayor from January 1991 to December 2003. During his long tenure, he promoted continued efforts to preserve the historical integrity of landmarks in Denham Springs. In 1995, he announced the creation of the Denham Springs Historic Preservation Commission, which held its first meeting on April 3, 1995. Delaune and the commission prioritized that the boundaries for the downtown historic district and preservation of Old City Hall take precedence.

James E. Durbin serves as the current mayor, from January 2003 to the time of this book's publication. Durbin is a lifelong resident of Denham Springs. Considered a hands-on mayor, he has overseen the city's residential growth, commercial expansion, infrastructure improvements, and profitable forecast. Durbin maintains an open-door policy of transparency in his administration. He presided over the city's centennial celebration in 2003.

Seen here is the induction of new members to the Masonic Lodge in 1971. (Courtesy of the Louisiana Masonic Library and Museum.)

Four
CLASSROOMS AND CHARACTERS

Mrs. E. Perie's 10th-grade class at Denham Springs High School poses in front of the school on January 6, 1921.

Hurricane Betsy wreaked massive damage across the entire southern region of Louisiana in 1965. The hurricane was the first in the Atlantic Basin to cause $1 billion in damage. The band room of Denham Springs High School experienced damage from the Hurricane.

Pictured here is the Denham Springs High School football team in 1930. The high school has served students of the community since 1912. This was the first organized football team to represent the high school. It was led by coach C.G. Hornsby, and their first game was against Donaldsonville High School on September 26, 1930.

This image was captured from the Denham Springs Carnival Ball in 1961. The carnival begins on Twelfth Night (January 6) and extends until Mardi Gras, the day before Ash Wednesday. Although the largest celebrations are held in New Orleans, 90 miles away, the community of Denham Springs also celebrates this season.

Another group of dancers celebrates at the Denham Springs Carnival Ball in 1961. Note the pairs of couples holding hands on the dance floor.

These schoolchildren perform a recital in May 1957. Proud mothers sit in a row to the right of children dressed in vibrant costumes.

Posing for the camera in what looks to be a salon are, from left to right, (first row) Ruth Ella Chambers, Kenelly Lamm, and Margaret Nabors; (second row) Lucille Richard Monroe, Pearl Guidry Hood, and Melba Nabors.

Denham Springs Collegiate Institute was established in 1895. It was a college preparatory, privately owned school that attracted many instructors from across the country. In 1908, the board of directors deeded the land to the public school system, and Denham Springs High School was built in 1910. The high school burned down in a fire that destroyed the entire campus in 1961. Pictured here are the remains of the building after the fire.

Denham Springs High School was established in 1897 and in 1910 moved to a two-story building on Main Street on land once occupied by Denham Springs Collegiate Institute. Seen here is the current campus of the high school on Range Avenue. It is one of nine high schools in Livingston Parish and is fed by the freshmen school and three other junior high schools in the area. Enrollment at the high school was 1,346 as of August 2010.

Denham Springs Junior High School, located on Hatchell Lane just north of the railroad tracks, is one of three feeder schools for Denham Springs High School.

In 1908, the board of directors of Denham Springs Collegiate Institute donated its land to the public school system. Pictured here in 1927 is the high school built on that land. (Courtesy of Mabel and Alec Pirie.)

The first "colored" school, the Brandon School, was established in 1907. Located on Hummel Street in 1914, it was moved to Roberts United Methodist Church, and in 1920 the Livingston Parish School Board appropriated $500 and built the Rosenwald School. In the 1950s, the African American schools were consolidated, and West Livingston High School was established in Denham Springs. The school was located on Rodeo Road and is now occupied as the Lockhart Community Center, pictured here. (Courtesy of Arthur Perkins.)

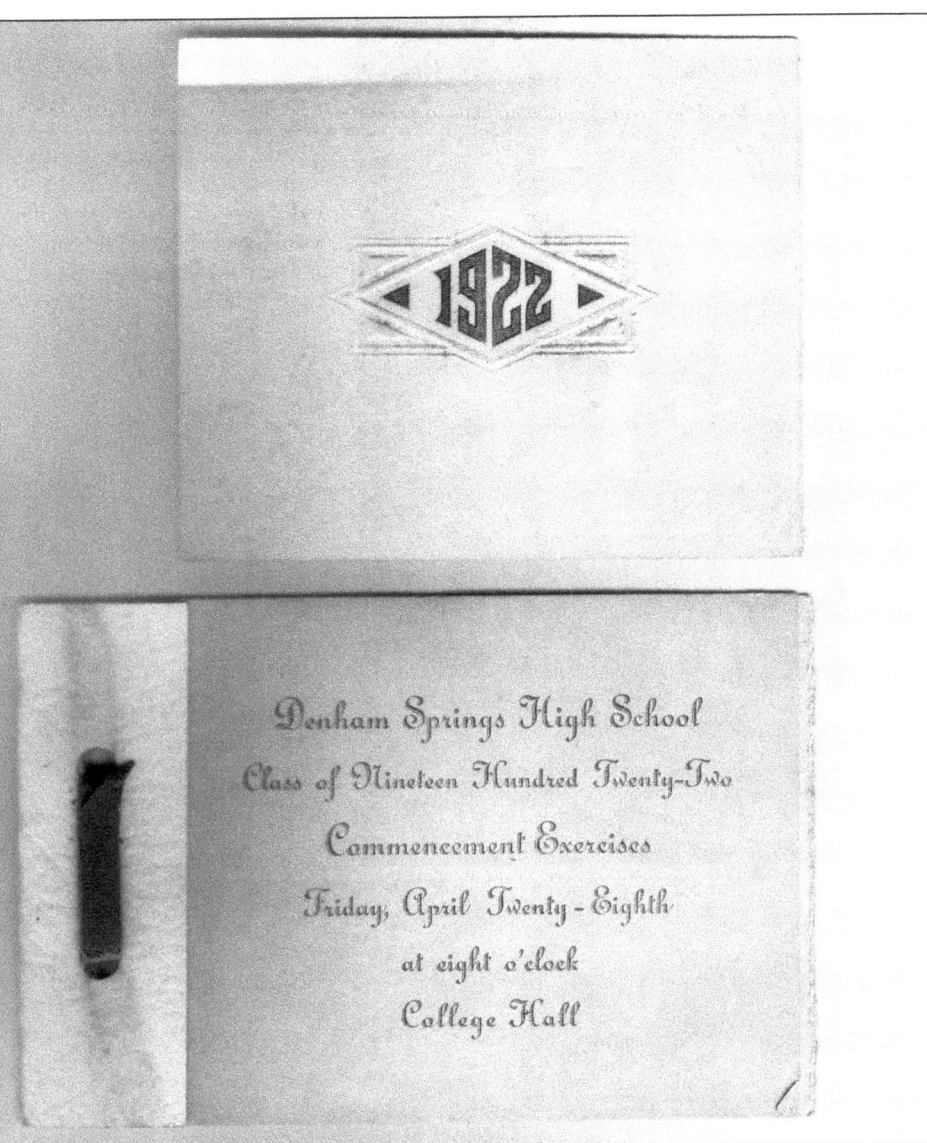

This is an invitation for the commencement ceremony of Denham Springs High School's class of 1922.

Esna Easterly poses here on March 7, 1955. Esna was married to Ernest Easterly Sr., who was superintendant of schools for Livingston Parish (from 1920 to 1929, 1937 to 1946, and 1955 to 1961). Esna was an eighth-grade teacher at Denham Springs Junior High School.

A young Donna Benton plays in her father's car in 1957. This photograph was taken at Cecil Benton's house on Cedar Street. (Courtesy of Donna Benton.)

Pictured from left to right are Leslie, Milton, Bill, Carey, and Earle Benton. Earle is the current owner of Benton Brothers Antiques, located in the antique district. (Courtesy of Bill Benton.)

Students cross the street in time for class at Denham Springs High School, located at the corner of Range Avenue and Yellow Jackets Boulevard. This photograph was taken in 1960.

This is a typical scene along Hummel Street in the 1950s. Here, two boys walk home from school wearing their Boy Scouts of America uniforms. (Courtesy of Pauline Barnett Stafford.)

Members of the starting backfield seen here pose during football practice at Denham Springs High School. These boys were on the 1961 team. From left to right are Jim Glass (halfback), Jim Spring (center), Charlie Causey (quarterback), David Hoffman (fullback), and Leo Kinchen (halfback). (Courtesy of Jim Spring.)

In this photograph taken during a 1957 football game is the coaching staff of the high school team. Seated from left to right are Dr. David Thibodeaux (team doctor), assistant coach Horace McCann, assistant coach Jim McCaleb, and head coach Charles Borde. (Courtesy of Jim Spring.)

Pictured are the queen and maids of the annual junior high school carnival in 1958. From left to right are Ann Spring, Diane Eisler, Sandra West, Queen Carolyn Comeaux, Linda Robinson, Sandra Smith, and Donna Lynn Felps. (Courtesy of Jim Spring.)

Denham Springs Freshmen High School, established in 1998 and originally the junior high, is the primary feeder school, along with the new Denham Springs Junior High School, for the high school. The campus pictured here is located on Range Avenue across the street from the high school, built in the early 1960s.

Mrs. Jackson's class poses in front of the Old Grammar School, built in 1927. The school replaced Denham Springs Collegiate Institute, which was located on River Road and North College Drive.

Five

OFF TO WORK, OFF TO WAR

Many young men were drafted and sent to fight and defend the United States in World War II. In this official US Navy portrait is local serviceman Guy Miller. (Courtesy of Ann Fugler.)

Following the Japanese attack on Pearl Harbor, the United States entered World War II. Boys boarded a bus on Range Avenue in the center of town and headed for Fort Polk in Leesville, Louisiana, to enter basic training after being drafted into the army. These boys from across America were sent to fight both the Nazis in Germany and naval forces of Japan.

John Hughes (left) and Robert Miscar pose in their uniforms from overseas, serving in the US Army in France during World War I.

Five men from Denham Springs pose in their uniforms before shipping off to Europe to fight in France on the Western Front in World War I. This is a typical image of local young men, demonstrating the widespread impact the war had on all Americans.

Pictured here are Bill Barnett and his wife, Birdie, outside an oil drilling well just north of Denham Springs. Birdie often came at lunchtime to bring her husband meals and snacks. The town discovered an oil shale in 1902, primarily in the village of nearby French Settlement, but the wells dried up by World War II. The drilling went to a depth of about 500 feet, producing several million barrels of crude oil over the life of the well.

This is a c. 1935 photograph of Jimmy Barnett (far left) and others at the end of their shift at the oil drilling well north of Denham Springs.

The Denham Springs Selling Association, established and owned by Manson Cockerham, represented merchants along Range Avenue. In this photograph, standing behind the counter to the left is local businessmen Homer Chambers (left) and Robert Benton (right). Chambers and Benton were successful business owners who promoted commerce in Denham Springs. This is a typical general store located on Range Avenue near the railroad depot. (Courtesy of Robbie Allen Spangler.)

Dr. T. Waldo Morgan served Denham Springs as dentist for 51 years. He came to Denham Springs from Baton Rouge and opened his first office in the old theater building on Range Avenue in the 1930s. He served on the city council for 10 years and was the utility commissioner for eight years.

Willie Guidry (left), the local blacksmith, is seen here with an unidentified man in front of his shop located at Mattie and Benton Streets.

Pictured here in 1938 in Brown's Oar Factory are, from left to right, Cecil Benton, Brady Brown, George Mansur, and Skeet Brown. They hold samples of the oars made at the factory.

The farmhouse of Edward Coleman Benton was located south of the town center on Range Avenue. Like most early families, Benton lived and operated a farm; he was also local blacksmith. Note that the dirt road in the photograph above is what is now the four-lane Range Avenue.

Among the helpful programs of Franklin D. Roosevelt's New Deal, the WPA funded construction of a city hall for the town of Denham Springs. The building was completed on November 21, 1940, and opened to the public for tours. Mayor Gay Cooper praised the quality and style of the building, and for the first time Denham Springs had a dedicated structure to house the mayor's office, police headquarters, library, jail, and courtroom. It is pictured here as it stands today. It was restored in 2009 and now serves as the city museum. Efforts for the restoration of Old City Hall began in 1995 under the mayoral auspices of James Delaune and completed during the mayoral guidance of James Durbin.

Pictured here from left to right are Sonny, Billy, and Ned Benton. These three brothers express the love that young men have for their siblings. They don the typical men's fashion of the 1950s. (Courtesy of Bill Benton.)

Men are seen working in Brown's Oar Factory. Willis Corbett Marsh (front right) holds the saw. The factory was the first of its kind in Louisiana and employed over 50 percent of the men in Livingston Parish. (Courtesy of Donna Benton.)

This is a group of oar finishers who worked at Brown's Oar Factory. They are posing outside the original factory before it burned down. The men oftentimes worked next door at the local sawmill for extra work and pay.

The Williamson family arrived in Denham Springs around 1909. Pictured here are Carolyn and Elvy Williamson with their two children, Richard (left) and James. Elvy and his two sons were prominent local businessmen in the Denham Springs community. (Courtesy of the Williamson family.)

In this photograph is one of the many coal locomotives that often stopped at the depot in Denham Springs. Many travelers came to the area by train to visit the mineral springs. The completion of the Baton Rouge, Hammond and Eastern Railroad spawned significant development in Denham Springs; it was the lifeblood of early commerce in the growing town. Local farmers and businessmen came to Denham Springs to sell their produce and supplies, including lumber, strawberries, and sweet potatoes. The depot led to the development of the Denham Springs Farmers' Association that bought crops and resold them to vendors across the Gulf South, transporting them via rail. Today, trains no longer stop in the city along these rail lines. (Courtesy of Clark Forrest.)

Wilfred Spring served in World War II. He rose to the rank of petty officer first class in the US Navy. After the war, he worked in Baton Rouge but eventually served as Denham Springs fire chief during the 1960s and 1970s. (Courtesy of Jim Spring.)

Six
Parks and Recreation

This is the beautifully landscaped site of the old railroad depot in downtown Denham Springs. Train Station Park, located downtown on Railroad Avenue, is the venue for numerous outdoor activities and events. It is not uncommon to see dancing in the street during many of these occasions. During the annual spring and fall festivals, the city hosts the popular pet costume and talent contest.

This mural is located along a fence at Springs Park on Tabernacle Road. Local artist Katherine Atchison completed it in 2004. The mural shows the artist's rendition of the springs and the Springs Hotel that once stood on the ridge overlooking the area.

The pavilion bandstand is located at Springs Park on the ridge overlooking the springs and nature trail. Operated by the city, the pavilion hosts many outdoor concerts and events.

This mural along a fence at Springs Park of a flow well from 1915 was part of a school art project. The flow well was a public drinking fountain from the mineral springs.

The Tastee Freez soda and ice cream shop served the families and youth of Denham Springs for over 20 years. Often the site of joyous children and overly energetic teenagers, Tastee Freez was the local hangout for the entire community.

The Amite River was once a source of local fish in great abundance when this image was captured on May 10, 1935. Pictured in front of James Drug Store are, from left to right, Bill Lamm, Walter Vincent, Martin Naul, Gay Cooper, and D.E. Coyle.

Mineral water springs come to the surface at the base of a low-lying ridge. These springs run through the center of the city and have figured in the city's name since at least the 1850s. Many people believed the springs to have curative properties; New Orleans publication *Men and Matters* promoted the health-restoring benefits of the spring water in a 1902 article on Denham Springs. One of the few remaining springs is pictured here. Note the high water from flooding of the Amite River.

The Kidz Korner Playground opened in 2010 as part of the city's efforts to provide clean and safe parks for children and their families. The park is located at the corner of River Road and Government Street. It was established as a coordinated effort between the Pilot Club of Denham Springs Foundation and the City of Denham Springs.

The Heard brothers built the Carol Theater in 1926. The first film featured was *Birth of a Nation*; they screened it in a hardware store across the street to determine if there was enough interest to support the building of a theater.

The City of Denham Springs enacted a program of historic preservation and park creation under the auspices of Mayor James Durbin. Among the many parks established, Sanctuary Park was completed in 2010. It is adjacent to the Old City Hall museum on the corner of Mattie and Benton Streets, which was once occupied by the fire department. This park is tranquil and features a live oak tree over 200 years old and iron benches for relaxing and reading on a beautiful day.

Seven
COMMERCE AND DEVELOPMENT

This is the old train depot truck loading dock at Range Avenue. During the first 50 years of the town, Denham Springs thrived as a depot for the delivery and hauling of various local crops, including lumber and strawberries. The railroad hauled lumber from oak and pine trees, as well as strawberries and satsumas from local farms across Livingston Parish.

Seen here is the old train depot housing station. From the 1910s to 1950s, the majority of farm and lumber supplies were loaded onto trains. The rail tracks once belonged to the Illinois Central Railway Co., which is now owned and operated by Canadian National Railroad. The housing station held the radio and telegraph for official railway business. Note Range Avenue crossing the rail tracks.

The old National grocery store was located on the corner of US Route 190 and Hummel Street. This was the first modern shopping center in the town, built in the 1950s. In the foreground is Claude Villar's 1977 Chevrolet Malibu.

Originally owned by the Barnetts, this Esso gas station, located east of Denham Springs, was on Highway 16 and Pete's Highway. The Barnums purchased this station and operated it from 1955 to 1980s. Esso would later be renamed the Exxon Oil Company.

Powers Drug Store supplied and served the people of Denham Springs from this building on the corner of Benton and Centerville Streets. The drugstore shared this property with the Masonic Lodge, which served the Masonic brethren of the village. The building was erected in 1914, nine years after the establishment of the local charter of the Masonic Order. It was demolished in 1971. Powers Drug Store ceased to operate, and the Masonic Order opened a new building.

Ruth and James Carter originally opened the Whistle Stop Café in 1995. It was built in the design of the old train depot that stood next to the railroad tracks. Kristine Bajon has currently operated it since October 2012. The Whistle Stop Café serves gourmet coffee, sandwiches, and cake balls to its customers.

Brignac Used Cars operated and served the people of Denham Springs from 1949 to 1977. It was located on Hatchell Lane near US Route 190 in the area known as Dodge City.

Pictured here is Barnett's Store around 1955. Barnett's served as a local grocery for the community of Denham Springs for several decades. It was located on the corner of US Route 190 and Hatchell Lane. Barnett's gas station opened in 1946, and in 1955 it was converted into a grocery store. Note the extension of the awning and removal of the fuel pumps.

Texan William Brown partnered with local sawmill owner Jim Benton and built the first factory in Denham Springs. Brown's Oar Factory was dedicated to the fabrication of wooden oars using the lumber from Benton's sawmill. In 1912, the factory burned down, and the second structure was built along the railroad at River Road. The sawmill and factory established a successful business that employed the majority of men in Denham Springs. Pictured here is Brown's Oar Factory in 1949.

The corner of Centerville Street and Range Avenue is seen here after the rain during the flood of 1955. Vance's Esso gas station occupied the corner. Note the automobile parked on higher ground close to the building.

Pictured here is the oldest standing building in the city of Denham Springs. This structure housed the first real estate office, savings and loan, and bank. Today, it is occupied by a local consignment shop.

The People's Bank of Denham Springs was built in 1903. The structure later housed the Bank of Denham Springs, several real estate offices, and a library. The bank is seen here after its completion in 1903.

Seen here is the newest building erected in the city (at the time of publication), located on the corner of Range Avenue and Centerville Street. This structure was built in the Art Deco style similar to the state capitol building in nearby downtown Baton Rouge. It was constructed and designed for a bank that has not yet opened for business.

Bass Pro Shops's construction was completed in 2005. As one of the largest branches of the Missouri-based chain of stores, this local business brings customers and tourists from across Louisiana and the Gulf Coast region to Denham Springs each year.

John and Michelle Cavalier opened a business in 2005 to help public schools acquire necessary books to operate. On September 5, 2009, they opened Cavalier House Books in this quaint shop among the antique stores and shops of Denham Springs. Today, Cavalier House Books is a staple and treasure to readers of all ages in the community.

Benton Brothers Furniture was originally called Four B Sales. Four Benton brothers started the first furniture business of Denham Springs that served the community. Earl Benton now operates an antiques store in this former furniture store. His business is the oldest of several antique stores in the downtown Antique District.

Sam's Club opened in the summer of 2012, providing bulk-packaged products to the communities of Livingston Parish. The introduction of Sam's Club indicates the direction of economic growth in Denham Springs. The store is located next to Bass Pro Shops on Bass Pro Shops Boulevard.

The Old Hotel, located on Range Avenue, hosted many overnight guests during its tenure. It was the first building in Denham Springs to have a working mechanical elevator. The hotel is now occupied by Crowder Antiques and run by Florence Crowder, which sells high-quality antique items, from silverware to furniture.

Seen here in the 1950s in front of an advertisement for Brown's Oar Factory are descendants of William Brown. Members of the Brown family are, from left to right, John Allen, Lucille Brown, Maxie Lee Dixon, John Thomas Brown, Maurice Cockerham, Jim Brown, Dinnie Brown, Kathy Brown, Lela Brown, Bill Brown, Mike Brown, Marie Brown, and Billy Brown.

This is an advertisement of the Denham Springs Motor Co., which sold Ford Model T automobiles and was located on the corner of Centerville and Hummel Streets. (Courtesy of Carol Lamm.)

Bill's Bargain Barn served the community for all its general-purpose needs for many years. Bill Benton, owner and operator, is seen here in front of his store on the corner of Hummel and Centerville Streets. (Courtesy of Bill and Bettye Benton.)

Pictured here is a vintage label on a storage barrel that was once at the Denham Springs Farmers' Association before being loaded on a rail car and shipped across the country. Here, barrels of local sweet potatoes were grown and brought from farms around Livingston Parish. (Courtesy of Clark Forrest.)

Occasionally, rains come down for extended periods, and flooding occurs along the Amite River. More rare are the occasions when river waters rise to flood the entire town center. This is a picture taken of Centerville Street during the flood of 1953.

This is an advertisement for locally grown strawberries. It is another example of the crops raised and sold throughout Livingston Parish. The advertisement was distributed at the Denham Springs Farmers' Association and is dated to 1925. Strawberries remain a primary crop grown throughout the parish and is featured and sold at the annual Louisiana Strawberry Festival in Ponchatoula, Louisiana. (Courtesy of Clark Forrest.)

Visit us at
arcadiapublishing.com